Thank you for purchasing a Joanie Boney book ☺

Printed in the USA

Joanie Boney Books are multicultural and multiracial
reflecting the true America.

Illustrated by Karen Codorniz

Uimpact Publishing LLC

I would like to know how much you liked my book
so please leave a review ☺

Dad's my Best BUDDY

Written by Joanie Boney
Illustrated by Karen Codorniz

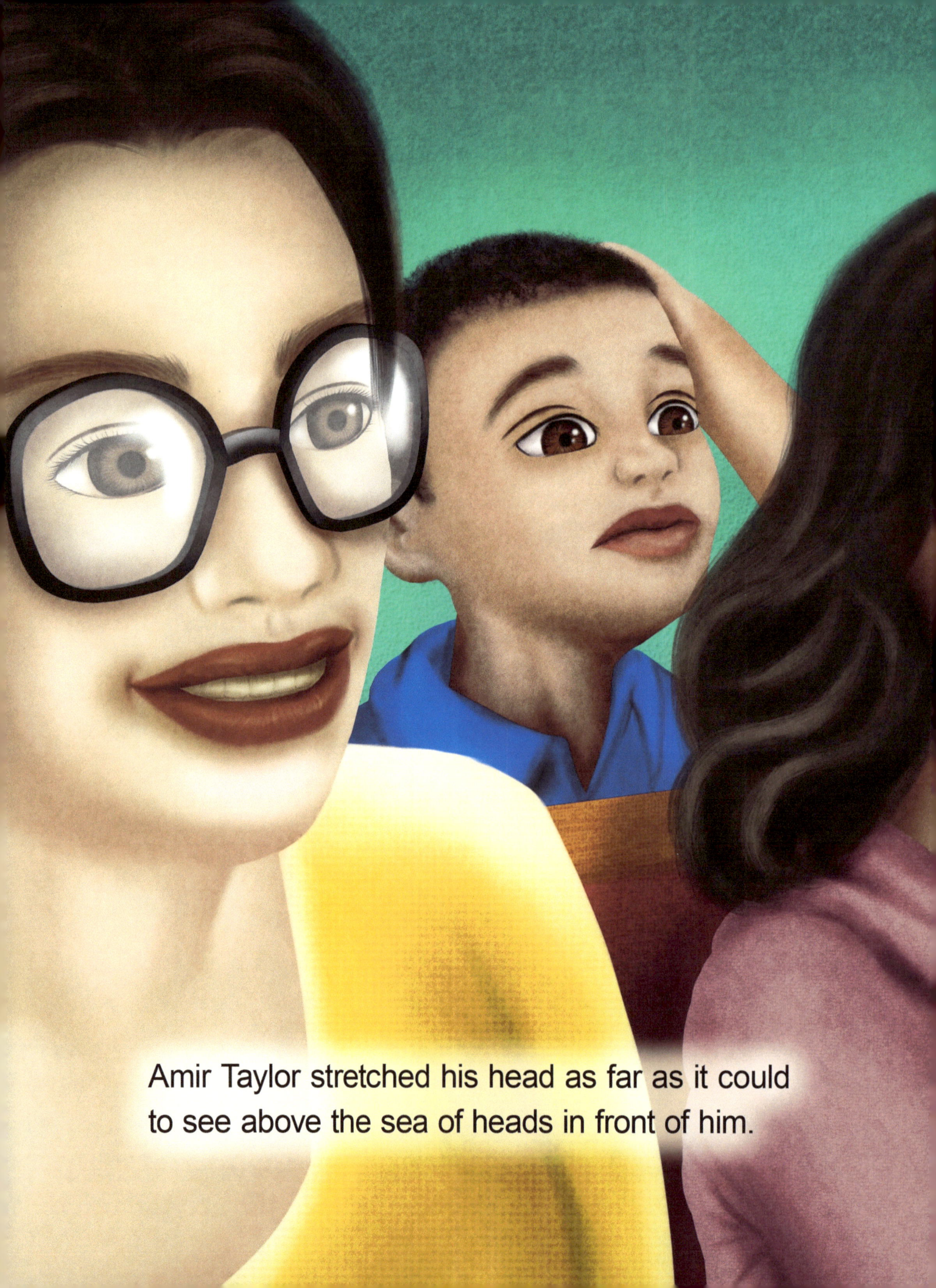

Amir Taylor stretched his head as far as it could to see above the sea of heads in front of him.

He tried standing on his chair but at 4' any chance of view was still impossible.

He slouched miserably and let out a deep sigh as he tried to figure out the best way to view the stage.

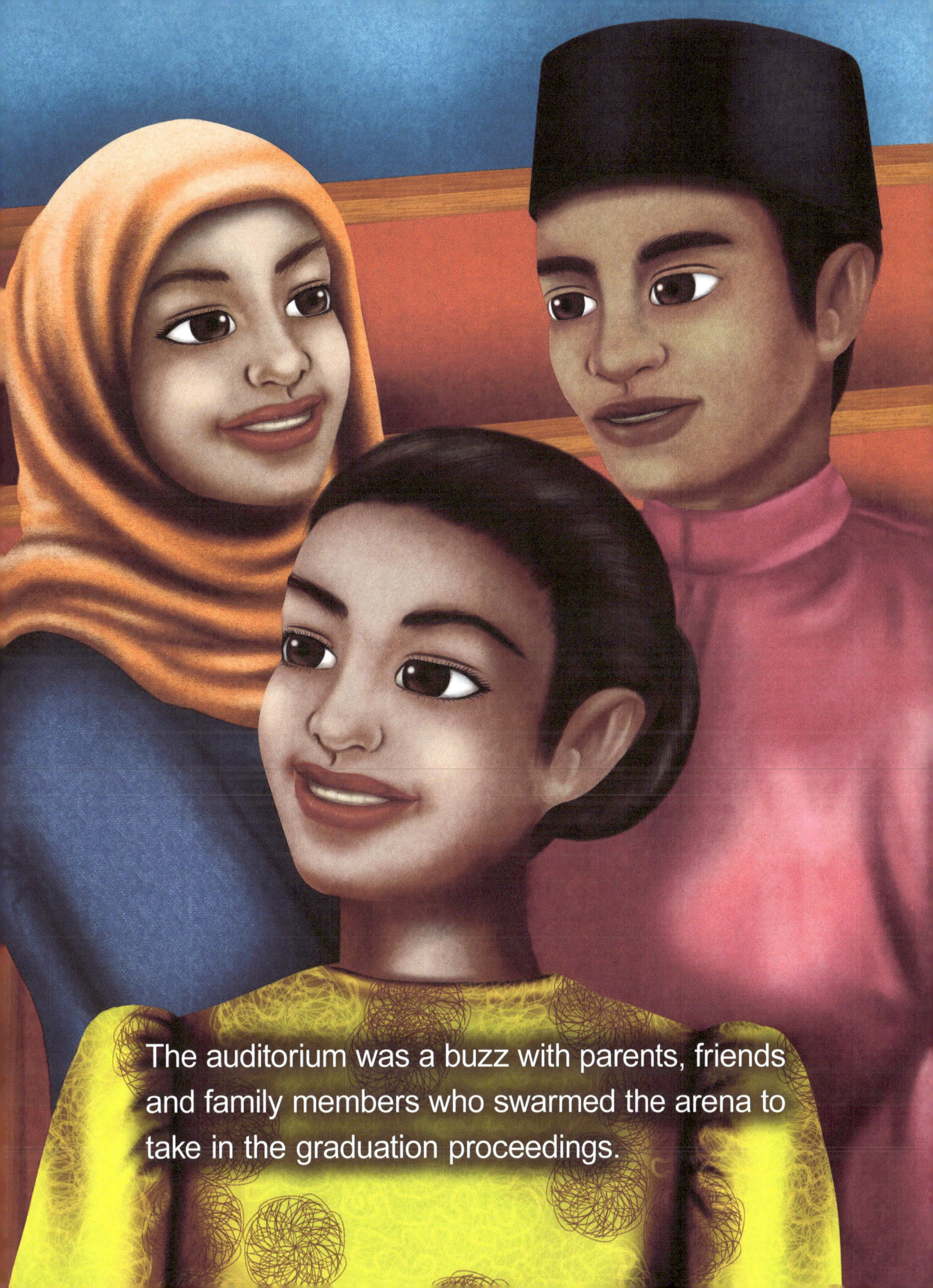

The auditorium was a buzz with parents, friends and family members who swarmed the arena to take in the graduation proceedings.

Little Amir was overwhelmed with all the chatter, flashing cameras and excited graduates.

"I can't see Mom…." Amir cried as he peered up at his mother with his big brown eyes.

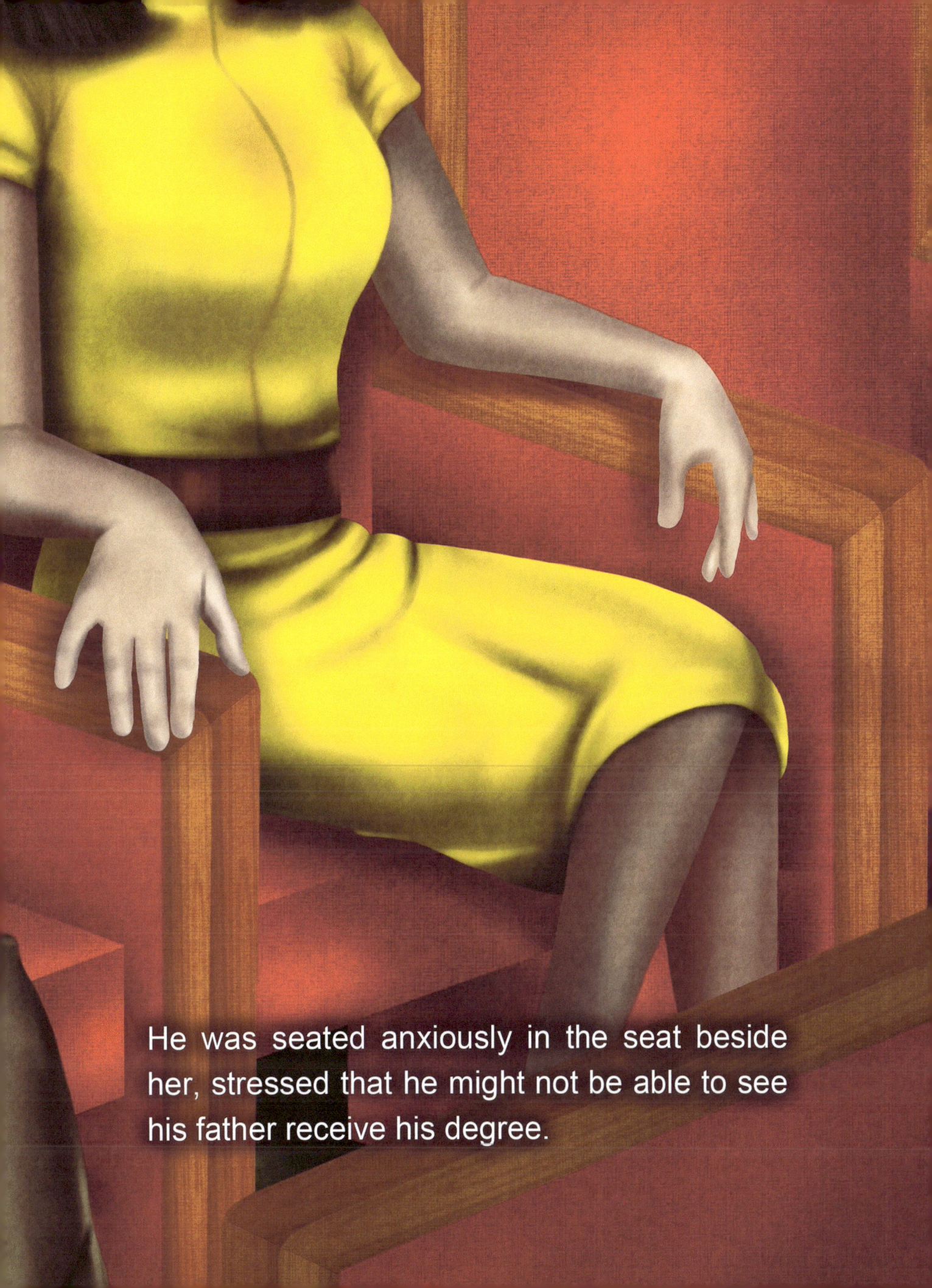

He was seated anxiously in the seat beside her, stressed that he might not be able to see his father receive his degree.

"Don't worry Amir.... We will see daddy when he comes on stage, I promise". Amir wasn't satisfied with his mother's reassurance.

There was no way he could miss seeing his father walking across the stage to collect his Masters degree in engineering. "Are you sure Mom? He asked again. "I'm sure honey, don't worry" she said lovingly.

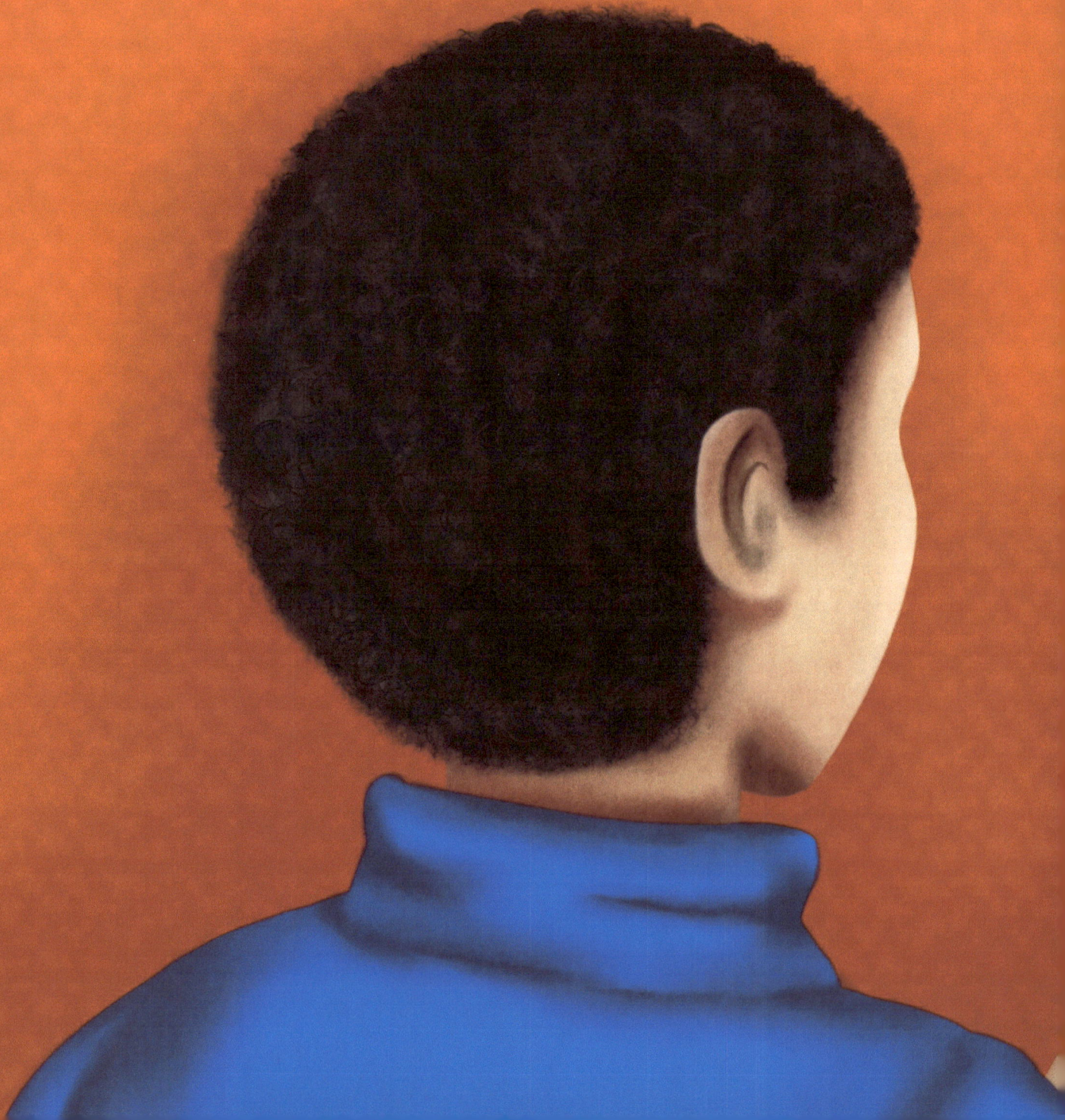

Amir's mother, Lillie stared in adoration at her son and smiled. She wasn't surprised that it was so important to Amir to see his father graduate.

Not only did he want to take pictures with his toy camera but Amir's daddy was his best buddy, his teacher and his role model.

Jordan and Lillie were lost. At 18 years old, Jordan and Lillie, fresh out of high school had no idea how to raise a child. Jordan, plans to attend Uimpact State University - his dream school and play college football took a drastic turn.

He traded in his allowance for a paycheck and ventured out to become the father his son needed. Jordan worked two jobs, one at a fast food joint and another at the corner garage.

Jordan turned his back on his teenage life of parties, video games. Instead he made sure to come home every night to help Amir with his homework, fix his dinner and tuck him into bed.

Pretty soon Amir and Jordan developed a special bond. They did everything together from visiting amusement parks, watching movies and going to basketball games. They were "two peas in a pod" – completely inseparable.

By the time Amir was 10 he was a bright, talented and active young boy. The top student in his class and involved in variety of activities, from karate, student government and soccer.

Jordan never missed a karate tournament, a soccer match or a school assembly. No matter how busy his schedule got he was always there for his son. He instilled in his son lessons of responsibility, determination and gratitude.

COMMUNITY
COLLEGE

As Amir grew up, Jordan realized the important role he was playing in his son's life. He took a few classes at the local community college.

Lillie found those years to be the most difficult time in their family. Many times Jordan would come in exhausted from work, and insisted he help Amir with his homework, put him to bed and then go to his evening classes.

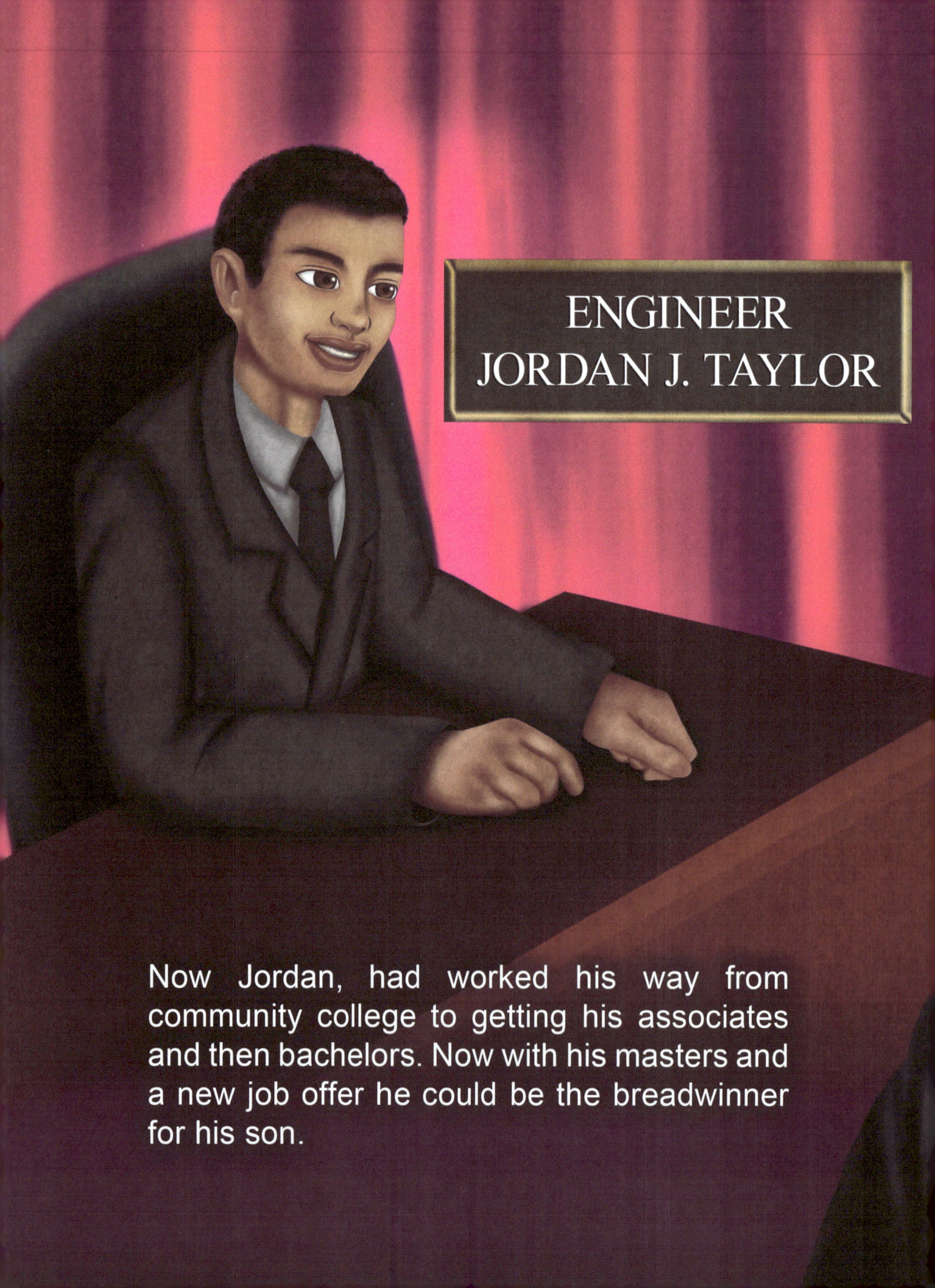

ENGINEER
JORDAN J. TAYLOR

Now Jordan, had worked his way from community college to getting his associates and then bachelors. Now with his masters and a new job offer he could be the breadwinner for his son.

Watching her husband graduate,
Lillie beamed with pride.

Lillie felt a tug at her side.
"Mom, I can't see I'm going closer."

Before Lillie could respond, Amir bolted from his seat to the front of the stage. The ceremony was well under way and the master's degree recipients for engineering were about to take the stage.

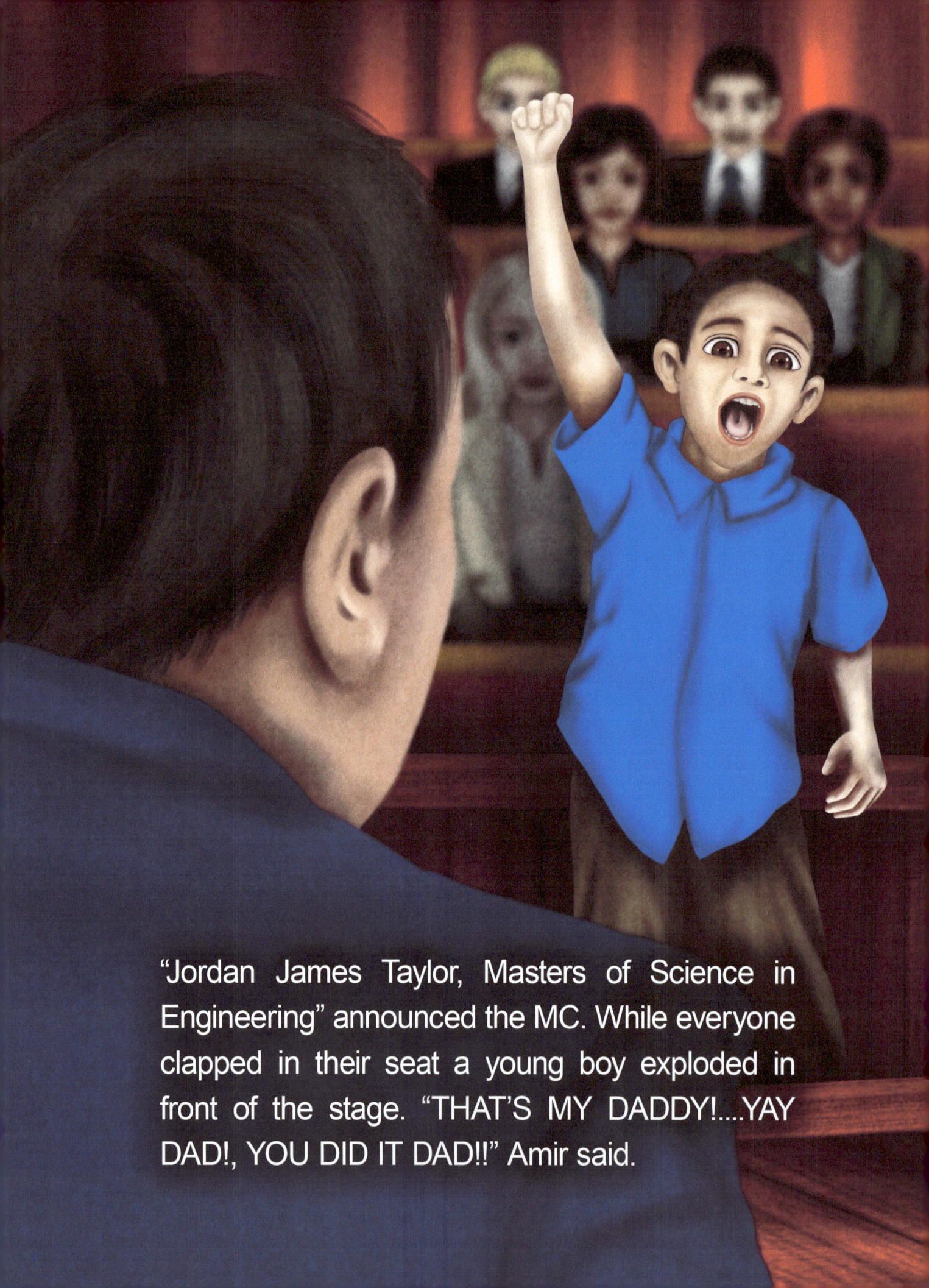

"Jordan James Taylor, Masters of Science in Engineering" announced the MC. While everyone clapped in their seat a young boy exploded in front of the stage. "THAT'S MY DADDY!....YAY DAD!, YOU DID IT DAD!!" Amir said.

As Jordan reached the other end of the stage, a small tear escaped his cheeks. Amir had become his biggest supporter and cheered for him the same way he cheered at his Soccer games.

He realized he had made his son proud and that despite their setbacks, he became the role model his son needed.

The Beginning
of a beautiful family.

THE END